CONTENTS

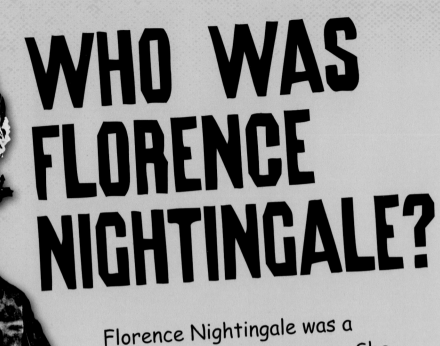

WHO WAS FLORENCE NIGHTINGALE?

Florence Nightingale was a nurse in the 19th **century**. She is famous for helping **injured** soldiers during the **Crimean War** and for her ideas about **nursing**.

This is a photograph of Florence Nightingale. Photography was a new invention in the 19th century.

FACT CAT

FLORENCE NIGHTINGALE

Izzi Howell

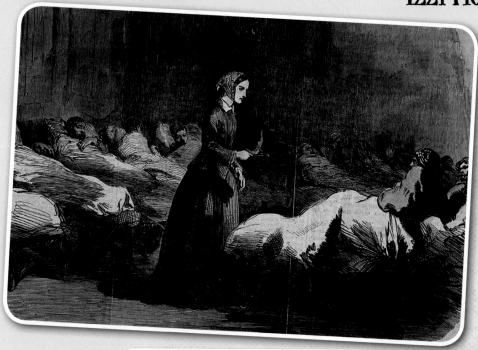

FACT CAT

Get your paws on this fantastic new mega-series from Wayland!

Join our Fact Cat on a journey of fun learning about every subject under the sun!

Published in paperback in Great Britain in 2018 by Wayland

Copyright © Wayland 2016

ISBN: 978 1 5263 0169 7

10 9 8 7 6 5 4 3 2 1

Wayland
An imprint of Hachette Children's Group
Part of Hodder & Stoughton
Carmelite House
50 Victoria Embankment
London EC4Y 0DZ

An Hachette UK Company
www.hachette.co.uk
www.hachettechildrens.co.uk

A catalogue for this title is available from the British Library
Printed and bound in China

Produced for Wayland by
White-Thomson Publishing Ltd
www.wtpub.co.uk

Editor: Izzi Howell
Design: Clare Nicholas
Fact Cat illustrations: Shutterstock/Julien Troneur
Other illustrations: Stefan Chabluk
Consultant: Karina Philip

Picture credits:
Alamy: Granger, NYC./Alamy Stock Photo 6 and 17 (b); iStock: BernardAllum 11 (t) and 19, duncan1890 11 (b); Mary Evans Picture Library: 7, 9, 10039147a 13, Grenville Collins Postcard Collection 14, 16; Shutterstock: Everett Historical title page (check), 10 inset, catwalker 17 (t), chrisdorney 21; Topfoto/The Granger Collection cover; Wellcome Library, London: 4, 5 and title page, 8, 12, 15, Science Museum/Wellcome Images 18, 20.

The author, Izzi Howell, is a writer and editor specialising in children's educational publishing.

The consultant, Karina Philip, is a teacher and a primary literacy consultant with an MA in creative writing.

FACT CAT FACT

There is a question for you to answer on most spreads in this book. You can check your answers on page 24.

At the time of the Crimean War, many **army** hospitals were dirty and dangerous. Florence worked to make the hospitals cleaner. This saved the lives of many **patients**.

Florence Nightingale was known as 'The Lady with the Lamp' because she carried a **lantern** when she checked on the soldiers in the hospital at night.

FACT CAT FACT

Florence worked up to twenty hours a day in the army hospital!

CHILDHOOD

Florence Nightingale was born on 12 May 1820 to a rich family. As a child, Florence didn't go to school. She was taught at home by her father. Her favourite subjects were history and maths.

FACT CAT FACT

Florence was named after the city of Florence in Italy, where her family were living when she was born. When Florence was one year old, her family moved back to England.

This is a portrait of Florence (standing) and her older sister. What was her sister's name?

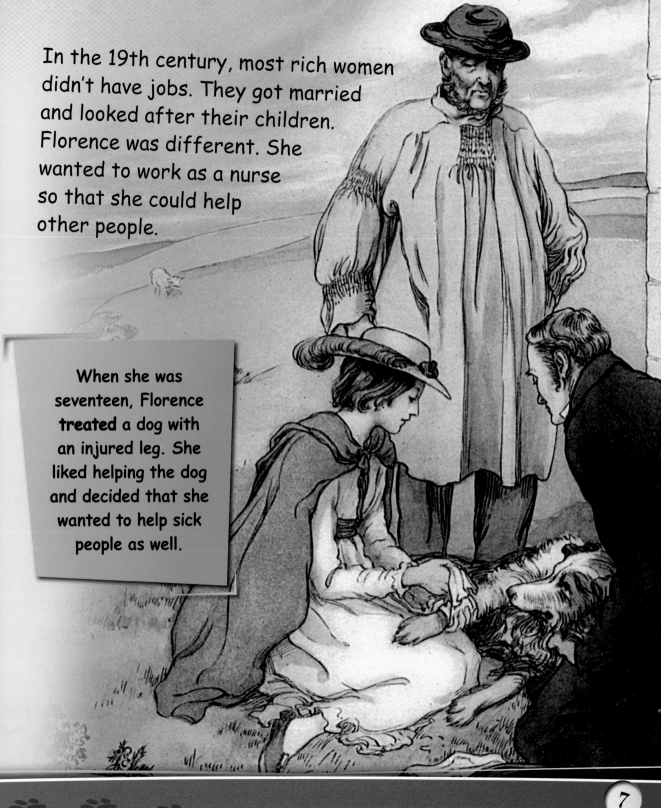

In the 19th century, most rich women didn't have jobs. They got married and looked after their children. Florence was different. She wanted to work as a nurse so that she could help other people.

When she was seventeen, Florence **treated** a dog with an injured leg. She liked helping the dog and decided that she wanted to help sick people as well.

BECOMING A NURSE

Florence's family were unhappy that she wanted to become a nurse. They didn't think that it was a suitable job for a woman from a rich family.

This 19th century cartoon shows a grumpy nurse. At that time, many people thought that nurses were lazy and badly behaved.

However, Florence did not listen to her parents. She went to Germany to study nursing for three months. Then, she found a job running a women's hospital in London.

Florence speaking to the doctors at the hospital she ran in London.

FACT CAT FACT

All the doctors at the women's hospital were men. In the 19th century, it was very difficult for a woman to become a doctor because people didn't think that it was a suitable job for a woman. Find out if men could work as nurses in the time of Florence Nightingale.

THE CRIMEAN WAR

The Crimean War started in 1853. Britain, Turkey and France fought against Russia in an area called Crimea.

This **modern** map shows Crimea where the Crimean War took place.

UKRAINE

MOLDOVA

RUSSIA

CRIMEA

GEORGIA

ROMANIA

Black Sea

BULGARIA

TURKEY

•Scutari

Great Britain

Crimea

Many soldiers were injured in battle. What types of weapons did soldiers use in the Crimean War?

The **conditions** on the Crimean War battlefields were very bad. The soldiers' camps were dirty and cold. Many soldiers caught a **disease** called **cholera** from drinking dirty water.

Sick and injured British soldiers waiting to be taken to hospital.

The hospital for British soldiers was not in Crimea. It was in the town of Scutari in Turkey. Soldiers had to travel across the Black Sea by boat to get to the hospital.

THE BRITISH HOSPITAL

It was hard for the sick and injured to **recover** at the hospital for British soldiers. There weren't enough doctors, beds or medicines. In Britain, people were shocked when they read about the hospital in newspapers.

This drawing shows a Russian army hospital during the Crimean War. The British hospital in Scutari looked very similar. Find three things that are wrong with the hospital in this picture.

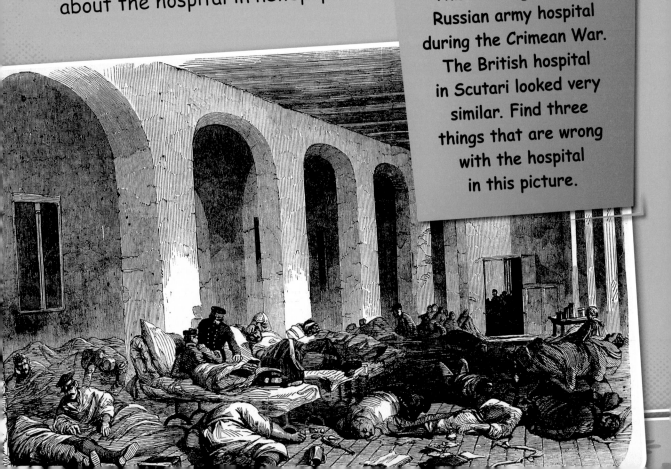

The **government** asked Florence Nightingale to run the hospital in Scutari and make it better. In 1854, she travelled to Turkey with a team of 38 nurses. However, at first, the doctors didn't allow the nurses to help.

Florence wasn't allowed to treat patients, so she prepared food for them instead. Florence paid for extra food herself to make sure that there was enough for everyone to eat.

FACT CAT FACT

When Florence Nightingale first arrived at the hospital, more soldiers were dying from diseases than from battle injuries.

MAKING CHANGES

Slowly, the doctors allowed Florence and the nurses to make changes. The nurses cleaned the hospital and gave each soldier clean clothes and a bed. Soon, Florence was running the hospital herself.

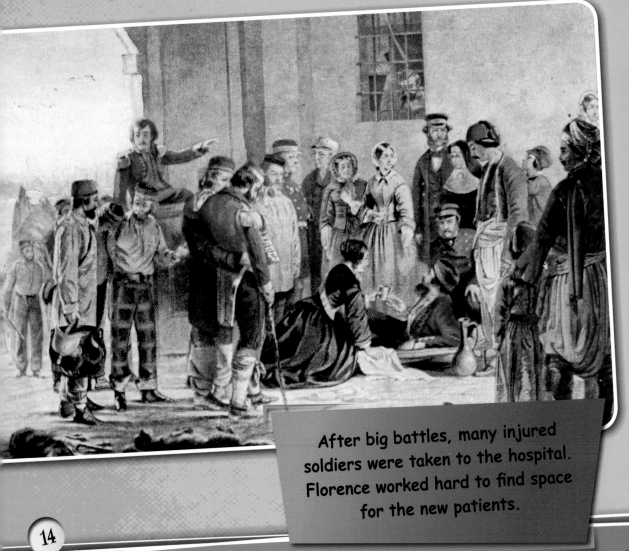

After big battles, many injured soldiers were taken to the hospital. Florence worked hard to find space for the new patients.

Florence also asked for the hospital **water supply** to be cleaned. There were cholera **germs** in the **pipes**, which made people ill when they drank the water. After it was cleaned, fewer people became sick in the hospital.

The British hospital after it had been cleaned. What differences can you see between this picture and the picture on page 12?

FACT CAT FACT

The soldiers in the hospital had a pet tortoise named Jimmy.

ON THE BATTLEFIELDS

Florence's hospital was far from the battlefields. Many injured soldiers died on the way to the hospital. Florence Nightingale decided to go to the battlefields to help the soldiers there.

Florence Nightingale travelled to the battlefields in a horse-drawn carriage.

Florence Nightingale wasn't the only nurse who worked in the Crimean War. A British Jamaican nurse named Mary Seacole set up a hotel for injured soldiers near the battlefields and saved many lives.

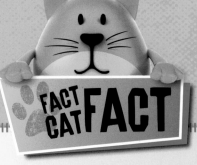

For many years after the Crimean War, the work of Mary Seacole was forgotten. Today, she is famous for her work in the war, along with Florence Nightingale. What is the name of the book that Mary Seacole wrote about her life?

1st

MARY SEACOLE
NATIONAL PORTRAIT GALLERY
2006

In 2006, a stamp showing a portrait of Mary Seacole was created to celebrate her life.

This nurse is helping soldiers on the battlefield.

COMING HOME

News of Florence's good work in Crimea travelled back to Britain. She became famous. Everyone was very grateful that she had saved so many lives.

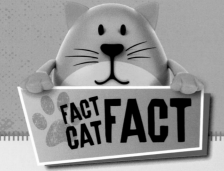

FACT CAT FACT

Florence hated being famous. She wanted to carry on with her work without lots of attention.

After Florence became famous, people bought paintings and ceramic souvenirs of her life.

MISS NIGHTINGALE

When the Crimean War ended in 1856, Florence returned to Britain. She taught other people about **hygiene** in hospitals. She also worked with the British Army to make all army hospitals cleaner and safer.

Florence Nightingale met Queen Victoria in 1856. The queen was very impressed with Florence's work.

LATER YEARS

Florence Nightingale became ill after working hard for many years. She wrote books about nursing while she was recovering. Later, she opened a school for nurses called the Nightingale School for Nurses.

Florence

Florence with student nurses at the Nightingale School for Nurses. At the school, nurses learned how to take care of patients and how to run a clean hospital.

Florence died in 1910 at the age of ninety. Thousands of people went to her funeral at St Paul's Cathedral in London. Today, she is remembered for helping to make hospitals cleaner and for changing people's ideas about nursing.

After her death, this statue of Florence Nightingale was put up in London to celebrate her life.

FACT CAT FACT

You can find out more about Florence's life at the Florence Nightingale Museum in London. The museum has a collection of objects that belonged to Florence, including her **stuffed** pet owl. What was her pet owl's name?

QUIZ Try to answer the questions below. Look back through the book to help you. Check your answers on page 24.

1 Florence Nightingale helped injured soldiers during the Crimean War. True or not true?

a) true

b) not true

2 In which country was Florence Nightingale born?

a) England

b) Italy

c) Germany

3 Florence went to work in the British hospital because she was bored in England. True or not true?

a) true

b) not true

4 Florence also helped soldiers on the battlefields. True or not true?

a) true

b) not true

5 What did Florence do after the Crimean War?

a) She worked as a nurse for Queen Victoria.

b) She got married and had children.

c) She worked with the British Army to make all army hospitals better.

GLOSSARY

army the soldiers that fight for a country on the ground

century a period of 100 years. The 19th century refers to dates between 1800 and 1899.

cholera a disease that comes from drinking dirty water

condition the situation that a person or place is in

Crimean War a war in which Britain, France and Turkey fought against Russia (1853–1856)

disease an illness

germs very small living things that cause disease

government the group of people who control a country

hygiene keeping things clean

injured hurt

invention something that has been designed or made for the first time

lantern a light that can be carried, often with a candle inside

modern describes something from the present

nursing the work done by nurses

patient someone who is being treated by a doctor or nurse

pipes tubes that bring water into a house or a building

recover to get better from a disease or an injury

stuffed when a dead animal is stuffed, its body is filled with a special material so that it keeps its shape for a long time

treat to care for someone or something with a disease or injury

water supply the water available in an area

INDEX

ANSWERS

Pages 6–21

Page 6: Frances Parthenope

Page 9: No, men did not work as nurses at this time.

Page 11: Swords and guns

Page 12: Some things include soldiers lying on the floor, no blankets, objects on the floor, no lights, windows closed.

Page 15: Some differences include soldiers in beds, clean blankets for all patients, windows open, light, no objects on the floor, spacious, nurses and doctors helping patients.

Page 17: Wonderful Adventures of Mrs Seacole in Many Lands

Page 21: Athena

Quiz answers

1   true

2   b - Italy

3   not true – she was asked to go because they needed someone to run the hospital and make it better.

4   true

5   c – she worked with the British Army to make all hospitals better.

Best Wishes John Potter Nov. 06.